Mutants in Nature

BY KIRSTEN W. LARSON

AMICUS HIGH INTEREST ✦ AMICUS INK

Amicus High Interest and Amicus Ink are imprints of Amicus
P.O. Box 1329, Mankato, MN 56002
www.amicuspublishing.us

Library of Congress Cataloging-in-Publication Data
Larson, Kirsten W., author.
  Mutants in nature / by Kirsten W. Larson.
     pages cm. – (Freaky nature)
"Amicus High Interest is an imprint of Amicus."
  Summary: "This photo-illustrated book for elementary readers
describes the types of mutations that can happen to animals
and plants. Highlights how outside forces or random genetic
mishaps can cause extra or missing limbs, color variations such
as albinism, and other abnormalities"– Provided by publisher.
  Audience: K to grade 3.
  Includes bibliographical references and index.
  ISBN 978-1-60753-780-9 (library binding)
  ISBN 978-1-60753-879-0 (ebook)
  ISBN 978-1-68152-031-5 (paperback)
  1. Mutation (Biology)–Juvenile literature. 2. Genetics–Juvenile
literature. I. Title.
  QH390.L37 2016
  576.5'49–dc23
                                          2014036515

Editor: Wendy Dieker
Series Designer: Kathleen Petelinsek
Book Designer: Heather Dreisbach
Photo Researcher: Derek Brown

Photo Credits: Alamy/Jim Zuckerman cover; Alamy/4nature.at
5; Alamy/Anna Curnow 10; Alamy/Arterra Picture Library 26;
Alamy/blickwinkel 9; Alamy/Exotic and Botanical - Chris Ridley
22; Alamy/Krys Bailey 28–29; Alamy/Shaun Cunningham 20;
Alamy/WENN Ltd. 13; Getty Images/Hans Surfer 15; Science
Source/James H. Robinson 16; Shutterstock/nobeastsofierce
6–7; Shuttershock/nodff 25; Shutterstock/reptiles4all 19

Printed in Malaysia

HC 10 9 8 7 6 5 4 3 2 1
PB 10 9 8 7 6 5 4 3 2 1

Table of Contents

What Is a Mutant?

A bomb goes off. Pow! The explosion causes a change deep inside Dr. Bruce Banner's body. He becomes the Hulk. Hulk is a mutant. He carries a mistake in his **genes**. Mutants are not just in comic books. In real life, mutations make strange plants and animals. Animals may grow body parts in crazy places. Plants turn weird colors.

A mistake in this deer's genes makes it half white.

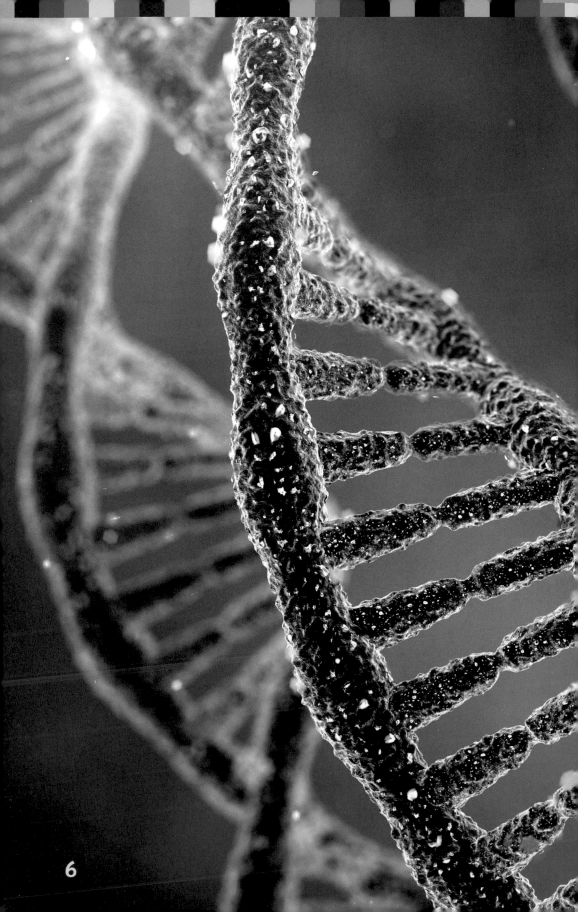

Cells are the building blocks of living things. They carry your genes. Genes are the directions for making living things. They help determine everything about you. They make you a boy or girl. They decide your hair and eye color. And when things go wrong with genes, strange things happen.

Genes are like a code for what you will look like. Sometimes that code can have mistakes.

7

Mixed-up Parts

A fruit fly grows legs on its head. Another gets an extra set of wings. Oops! Mistakes in "master" genes cause these mix-ups. The genes keep track of what body part to build as babies grow. The genes also know where and how to build the parts. When mistakes happen in master genes, parts can grow from the wrong spot. They can even be the wrong color or shape.

This fruit fly's eye is white because of a mix-up with its genes.

The same thing can happen in flowers. But people often find this mutation beautiful. Roses may grow with double flowers. The blooms do not have stamens and pistils. Instead, the plants grow extra petals. It looks like a flower growing within a flower. Roses often form double flowers. So do peonies and carnations.

This daffodil is growing with a double flower. How pretty!

In some places, cats with extra toes are common. Most cats have 18 toes. They have five toes on each front paw. Each rear paw has four. But in New England, many cats have extra toes. They may have six or seven on each paw. Cats with too many toes have been found in England and Florida, too.

 Which cat has the most toes?

These kittens were born with many extra toes. They have 54 toes between them!

 A cat named Jake has 28 toes. He has seven on each paw.

Sometimes animals have all their parts. The parts just do not grow right. Puppies are born with soft bones. Over time, their bones grow longer and harder. Some dogs may have a mistake that keeps their leg bones from growing long enough. Their legs are half the length of normal dogs.

 Which types of dogs have this problem?

This dog's front legs didn't grow to their full size.

 It most often affects bulldogs and German shepherds. Some dogs have been **bred** to have short legs, like dachshunds and Welsh corgis.

A half-sider butterfly has two sets of lovely colors.

 Q What other half-siders have been found?

Color Changes

In 2008, an Iowa gardener found an unusual butterfly. On its right side, it sported the bright orange colors of a male. On the left, it had the more subtle colors of the female. The butterfly was a rare mutant. Its genes were half male and half female. The animal is called a "half-sider."

 People have found insects, cardinals, chickens, and lobsters that are half male, half female.

Albinos look just like normal animals. There is one difference. They have white skin and pale pink or blue eyes. They carry a mistake that keeps their bodies from making color. Animals from people to penguins can be albino. It does not happen often. An albino alligator called Luna is one of 50 of her kind in the world. Wow!

 Can being albino cause problems for animals?

This albino aligator has a mutation. It does not have color like other aligators.

 Yes! Predators spot them easily. Then they become lunch. They also sunburn quickly.

What animal can be more unusual than an albino? How about a deer or squirrel with too much color? These animals have **melanism**. They look black or very dark. The mistake is common in some animals like moths. But it is rare in deer. In Texas, people found a black fawn. Yet both its mom and twin had normal colors.

This gray squirrel has too much color. It is black instead of gray.

This plant is a chimera, so its leaves are two different colors.

Q What are some other **chimeras**?

A pink flower grows a few white petals. When this mistake happens, it is called a chimera. In myths, a chimera was a monster made from parts of different animals. In a way, this flower is two different plants. One part has genes for pink flowers. The other has genes for white flowers. They grow side-by-side.

Apples may have sections of two colors. Plants with green leaves can have white spots or stripes.

Microscopic Mutations

You easily can spot many plant and animal mutations. But changes also happen in germs too tiny to see. Each year, cold and flu viruses make people sick. Achoo! But sometimes these viruses mutate into super bugs. Yikes! Then they spread very easily. They make many people sick around the world. In 2009, a mutated flu strain called the swine flu killed thousands of people.

This machine helps doctors test for germs and viruses to learn more about them.

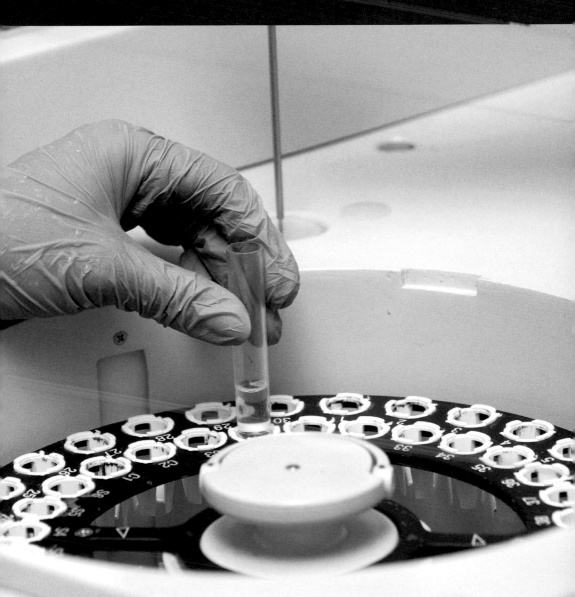

A mutation caused this chicken to grow two extra legs!

What Makes Mutations?

Mutations often happen on their own. But things outside the body cause problems too. **Radiation** from a bomb hit Hulk's cells. It caused his mutation. In real life, radiation from a 1986 explosion at a Ukrainian power plant created mistakes. Animals there have albino spots or strange-shaped body parts. People there got sick. Some even died.

No matter what causes mutations, they can make crazy creatures. A fly grows extra legs in its mouth! Or animals are born without color. These mistakes are all around us. You might see them at the zoo or aquarium. They even appear in comic books. Now that you have seen real mutants, Hulk may not seem so strange. Right?

A mistake in this blackbird's cells caused this lovely pattern.

Glossary

albino An animal or plant that cannot produce colors, animals have white skin and hair.

bred To have purposely chosen parents with certain traits so the children will have those traits as well.

cell A basic building block of plants and animals.

chimera A plant or animal that has two separate sets of genes in one body.

gene The part of a cell that gives directions for making a living thing.

melanism A change in an animal's genes that make the animal have too much color; they appear black or very dark.

radiation Rays of energy, such as light or heat; some kinds of radiation are harmful to living things and can cause mutations.

Read More

Boothroyd, Jennifer. *Eye Color: Brown, Blue, Green, and Other Hues.* Lightning Bolt Books: What Traits Are in Your Genes? Minneapolis: Lerner, 2013.

Racanelli, Marie. *Albino Animals.* New York: PowerKids Press, 2010.

Websites

American Museum of Natural History | The Gene Scene
www.amnh.org/explore/ology/genetics

Rare Dark Deer | Animal Oddities
blogs.discovery.com/animal_oddities/2010/09/rare-dark-deer-photographed-in-texas.html

White Wonders | National Geographic Education
education.nationalgeographic.com/education/news/white-wonders/?ar_a=1

Index

About the Author

Kirsten W. Larson used to work with rocket scientists at NASA. Now she writes about science for children. She's written more than a dozen magazine articles and several books for children. Her favorite part of writing this book was studying up on superheroes.